MW00782615

Kids learn best by doing...by experiencing things alongside the people they love and trust. My now young adult sons recall their favorite childhood memories of learning things at home with their family. Make Your House His Home offers creative, engaging ways to teach your kids profound lessons that will stick with them for a lifetime. I highly recommend this resource for families!

-**Monica Swanson**, author, and podcast host

Anchoring your heart in Scripture is one of the most important disciplines that leads to a flourishing life in Christ, not just for an adult, but especially for a child. However, many parents feel unqualified to lead their children spiritually and don't know how to let the word of God be a regular part of the conversion in their day to day family rhythms. In this book, Leah gives parents accessible, helpful, and easy to use tools to allow them to begin the discipleship process for their children where it bears the most fruit - in the home.

-**Wade Joye**, Worship & Church Coach, Consultant, and Speaker
Elevation Worship Pastor of 12 years

Make Your House His Home Is such a great tool in learning how to make Jesus the center of your family. Leah gives practical and fun ways to share the Gospel with your kids in an interactive way.

-**Tiffany Hudson**, Elevation Worship Leader & Songwriter

In a world where children are inundated with the immediacy of information, unrelenting stimulation, and a chaotic culture—*Make Your House His Home* is an oasis. Leah Langston helps parents to focus on what every child truly needs—the knowledge of God as their constant—and a path to a secure understanding of the Gospel message. With practical, fun, and easy-to-accomplish activities, this guide will provide parents with a blueprint for raising children with a Biblical worldview.

-**Sally Livingston**, LMFT, Parent Educator, and bestselling author of *Get Over It!: 4 Steps to Breaking Free from the Stuck Cycle*.

As a parent of 3 arrows (children) whose greatest sole desire since they took their first breath was that they would personally know & experience the love of Christ, I am so excited for the world to have *Make Your House His Home*. Leah gives us creative, fun, interactive ways to share the Gospel with our kids in tangible ways. Cultivating their faith is the greatest gift we can ever give them. I only wish I had it when mine were younger. Start sowing today!

-**Lilibeth Vilella**, Founder of @tiarasgirls, Teen royal conference rewriting the stats of teen suicide. Non-Profit Consultant & Exec Coach

Leah gives you the tools you need to creatively and practically engage your kids with the Word of God. There may not be a more important book you read.

-**Noah Herrin**, Pastor, Speaker & Christian Influencer

In an ever changing culture that's aggressively targeting our children, *Make Your House His Home* is a wonderful book you can use as a tool for equipping your child with truth through these lessons. The hands on participation not only inspires creativity, but will leave your child remembering exactly what the lesson was about!

-**Laura Bangar**, Business & Leadership Coach, Rodan & Fields Top Tier Leader

Make Your House His Home is an inspiring work. The way that Leah has applied scripture with practice to help you navigate the complexity of parenting is not only smart but extremely helpful for any stage of your journey as a parent.

-**Stephen Brewster**, Nashville-based Leadership Coach & Podcast Host

In a world of cynicism and a regular sharing of grievances, it is refreshing to see a book on parenting by a young and vibrant mom, who is sharing her journey of creating a Christ-centered home with all of us. This is a book of contagious joy. Leah Langston is not sharing a theory, but rather is letting the world take a look at how she immerses her home with Scripture and a love for Jesus. Every Christian family should not only get this book, but apply Leah's principles and actions into the dynamics of your family routine and culture. I am thankful Leah has not kept this to herself, and chose to share a piece of her life with us. As her pastor, I can assure you that she is the real deal!

-**Dean Inserra**, Lead Pastor of City Church Tallahassee & Author

As first time parents, sharing the gospel in a practical way can be daunting. *Make Your House His Home* gives you the tools you need to creatively engage your kids in building biblical foundations from an early age. Leah shows us easy ways to experience the Gospel as a family.

-**Chris and Amanda Bristow**, Influencers & Founders of Shop Emma Blake

I'm excited for other Christian parents to have this book as a tool for sharing the Word of God with their kids! Leah's creativity and the way she pairs scripture with activities and conversation starters is genius. This is exactly the kind of resource parents like us need who aren't always sure what to say or how to answer the tough questions. Thank you, Leah, for creating this book. We can't wait to share it with our own kids!

-**Abby Flynn**, Christian Writer, Founder of the Joy Rally Podcast

As new parents raising godly children in an evolving world, we are so thankful for the tools Leah has provided in Make Your House His Home. This resource equips families to teach, enjoy, and experience the Word together—raising up the next generation to know, rely on, and continue to spread the Truth".

-**Jake & Gracie Bell**, Lifestyle Influencers & Parents

make your house His HOME

a guide for parents and children to experience scripture together

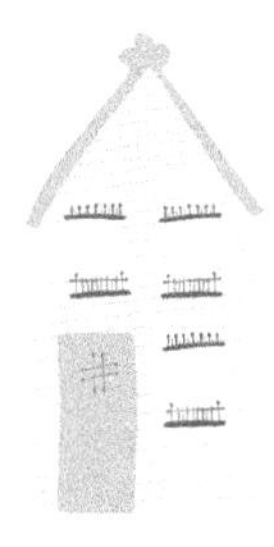
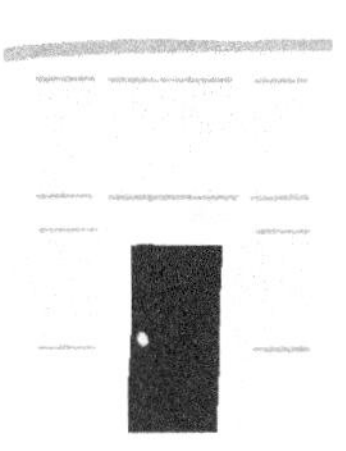

LEAH LANGSTON

Published by UNITED HOUSE Publishing

ISBN: 978-1-952840-24-1

UNITED HOUSE Publishing
Waterford, Michigan
info@unitedhousepublishing.com, www.unitedhousepublishing.com
Cover and interior formatting: Matt Russell, Marketing Image, mrussell@marketing-image.com

Published in Waterford, MI
Printed in the United States

2022—First Edition

To my boys, Luke and Levi, who I envisioned walking through each of these lessons with. I pray you grow more in love with God in every year of your life!

A Note to Parents

These lessons come to life only with your participation.
Set aside uninterrupted time to go through each activity.

Prepare

Read ahead so you can prepare and get creative.
Each lesson contains instructions for an activity you will need to plan.
Each lesson contains Bible scriptures to read and discuss with your children.

Participate

Bring the excitement. Make it an event. Make it "next level"
so your children understand and internalize the lessons.
Each lesson contains "The Big Picture"- what your children should
understand about God from the activities and scriptures.
And most importantly, channel that inner childlike faith.

It's most important they see the outlook and perspective you
have when reading because naturally, it's the outlook they will have, too!

Practice

Even though some of the lessons may seem elementary to adults, I pray that your faith is renewed in new ways as you move throughout this book. Because we too need to be reminded of these truths every day.

Table of Contents

In the Beginning

What You'll Need:

One bag per child (Ziploc, plastic, or anything will do!)

A yard, sidewalk, park—any space that features God's creation.

Instructions:

It's time to go on an epic nature walk!
Simply walk around your yard, down the sidewalk, or at your local park admiring all God has created. Isn't it EPIC?!?!
The goal will be to have the kids scout out and collect what they believe are the coolest things God created while on your walk.
As you walk, remind them God created everything they see; flowers, plants, trees, animals, humans—He made it all!

Head back to your home base with the items everyone has collected and have each person show the items found to the group, explaining why they love it. Study, name, and point out the details, admiring each masterpiece of God.

Scripture to Share:

In the beginning, God created the heavens and the earth. The earth was without form and void, and darkness was over the face of the deep. And the Spirit of God was hovering over the face of the waters.

And God said, "Let there be light," and there was light. And God saw that the light was good. And God separated the light from the darkness. God called the light Day, and the darkness he called Night. And there was evening and there was morning, the first day.

And God said, "Let there be an expanse in the midst of the waters, and let it separate the waters from the waters." And God made the expanse and separated the waters that were under the expanse from the waters that were above the expanse. And it was so. And God called the expanse Heaven. And there was evening and there was morning, the second day.

And God said, "Let the waters under the heavens be gathered together into one place, and let the dry land appear." And it was so. God called the dry land Earth, and the waters that were gathered together he called Seas. And God saw that it was good.

And God said, "Let the earth sprout vegetation, plants yielding seed, and fruit trees bearing fruit in which is their seed, each according to its kind, on the earth." And it was so. The earth brought forth vegetation, plants yielding seed according to their own kinds, and trees bearing fruit in which is their seed, each according to its kind. And God saw that it was good. And there was evening and there was morning, the third day.

And God said, "Let there be lights in the expanse of the heavens to separate the day from the night. And let them be for signs and for seasons, and for days and years, and let them be lights in the expanse of the heavens to give light upon the earth." And it was so. And God made the two great lights—the greater light to rule the day and the lesser light to rule the night—and the stars. And God set them in the expanse of the heavens to give light on the earth, to rule over the day and over the night, and to separate the light from the darkness. And God saw that it was good. And there was evening and there was morning, the fourth day.

And God said, "Let the waters swarm with swarms of living creatures, and let birds fly above the earth across the expanse of the heavens." So God created the great sea creatures and every living creature that

moves, with which the waters swarm, according to their kinds, and every winged bird according to its kind. And God saw that it was good. And God blessed them, saying, "Be fruitful and multiply and fill the waters in the seas, and let birds multiply on the earth." And there was evening and there was morning, the fifth day.

And God said, "Let the earth bring forth living creatures according to their kinds—livestock and creeping things and beasts of the earth according to their kinds." And it was so. And God made the beasts of the earth according to their kinds and the livestock according to their kinds, and everything that creeps on the ground according to its kind. And God saw that it was good.

Then God said, "Let us make man in our image, after our likeness. And let them have dominion over the fish of the sea and over the birds of the heavens and over the livestock and over all the earth and over every creeping thing that creeps on the earth."

So God created man in his own image, in the image of God he created him; male and female he created them. And God blessed them. And God said to them, "Be fruitful and multiply and fill the earth and subdue it, and have dominion over the fish of the sea and over the birds of the heavens and over every living thing that moves on the earth." And God said, "Behold, I have given you every plant yielding seed that is on the face of all the earth, and every tree with seed in its fruit. You shall have them for food. And to every beast of the earth and to every bird of the heavens and to everything that creeps on the earth, everything that has the breath of life, I have given every green plant for food." And it was so. And God saw everything that he had made, and behold, it was very good. And there was evening and there was morning, the sixth day.

Genesis 1:1-31 (KJV)

Questions to Discuss:

What is your favorite thing you collected? Why?

Why do you think God created so many different things?

How did God spend time creating these things?

How do you feel knowing God created you?

The Big Picture:

God is the Author and Creator.

He is the Beginning and the End.

He is in control of all things.

Prayer Time:

Encourage one member of your family to pray about the following:

-Thank God for the Six Days of Creation.

-Thank God for creating us!

-Ask God to show us how to admire His creation every day.

A Mighty Fortress

In this lesson, your children will understand God is our protector.
He is always there for us.

What You'll Need:

Sheet(s) or Blanket(s)
Pillows
Flashlights for an added experience

Instructions:

Use the sheet(s) or blanket(s) to create a fort in your house.
Allow your children to get creative with it—they can make the fort big, small, short, tall, but be sure the adult(s) can squeeze in the fort too.
Huddle underneath the fort to begin this study.

Scripture to Share:

The Lord is my rock and my fortress and my deliverer,
My God is my rock, in whom I take refuge;
My shield and the horn of my salvation, my stronghold.
Psalm 18:2 (NIV)

Questions to Discuss:

1. How do you feel sitting inside our fort?
2. Did you know you can talk to God any time you feel scared or unsafe?
3. Do you have anything you want to ask God to protect you from?

*Join in answering these questions too!

The Big Picture:

God is a mighty fortress. He is a safe place.
God is like a strong, unshakable castle.
God is our protection and shelter in times of trouble.

Prayer Time:

Encourage one member of your family to pray about the following:

- Thank God for being your safe place.
- Pray for the safety of each member of your family.
- Pray for protection over your home and your health.

The Armor of God

In this lesson, your child will understand that God is their protector.

What You'll Need:

Several rolls of aluminum foil

Instructions:

It's time to have a competition. Use aluminum foil to create "armor" for each person participating...full body armor! Allow others to rank each suit of armor and pick a winner! Have fun with it!

Scripture to Share:

Put on the full armor of God, so that you can take your stand against the devil's schemes. For our struggle is not against flesh and blood, but against the rulers, against the authorities, against the powers of this dark world and against the spiritual forces of evil in the heavenly realms. Therefore put on the full armor of God, so that when the day of evil comes, you may be able to stand your ground, and after you have done everything, to stand. Stand firm then, with the belt of truth buckled around your waist, with the breastplate of righteousness in place, and with your feet fitted with the readiness that comes from the gospel of peace. In addition to all this, take up the shield of faith, with which you can extinguish all the flaming arrows of the evil one. Take the helmet of salvation and the sword of the Spirit, which is the word of God.

Ephesians 6:11-18 (ESV)

Questions to Discuss:

1. Is there anyone who wears armor to do their job? Why?
2. What is the difference between armor and a fortress?
3. How would you feel if you were in full body armor?
4. Did you know God gives us His armor to wear each day? What does this look like?

The Big Picture:

God is our protector. He has given us His armor, and we can wear it every day.

Prayer Time:

Encourage one member of your family to pray about the following:

- Thank God for His protection.
- Thank God for preparing us for anything we may face with His Word.
- Ask God to teach us how to strengthen our spirits, our minds, and our bodies to fight for Him!

The Light of the World

In this lesson, your child will learn Jesus is our light in the world.
He will guide their path.

What You'll Need:

1 Candle, Flashlight, or Nightlight

Instructions:

Turn off all lights in the room (or house) and turn on a light of choice (candle, flashlight, or nightlight). Try walking around the house with the light in front of you. Encourage your children to envision Jesus just like the flashlight leading you through each step of darkness. After walking in the dark, initiate sitting around the light together.

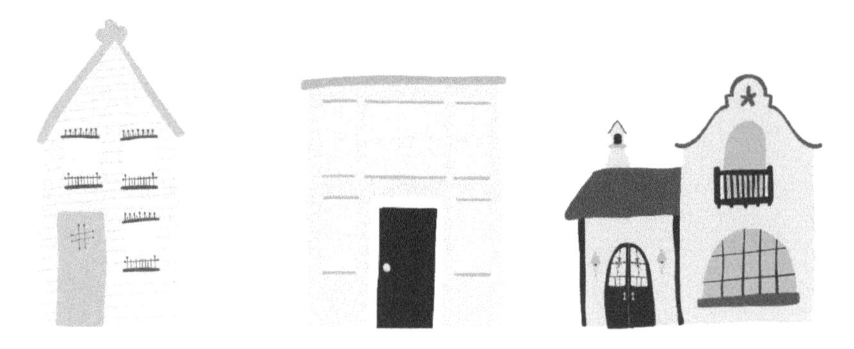

Scripture to Share:

Jesus spoke to them, saying, "I am the light of the world. Whoever follows me will not walk in darkness, but will have the light of life."

John 8:12 (ESV)

Questions to Discuss:

1. How do you feel when it's dark and you can't see?
2. Did you know God isn't afraid of the dark? Why not?
3. How does God light up our lives? The world?
4. Did you know you can be a light to others? How?

The Big Picture:

God is light.

If we follow him, He will light our path, and we will not walk in darkness.

He will be the light you need to take each next step!

Prayer Time:

Encourage one member of your family to pray about the following:

-Thank God for His Word.

-Thank Him for being your light, especially when we can't see clearly.

-Show us how to be a light to this world and those around us.

Go Fish!

In this lesson, your child will learn that they are called by Jesus to share Jesus with others.

What You'll Need:

All you need are yourselves for this one!

Instructions:

Think of this activity as a version of "follow the leader." As the adult, state that you will be the leader (at least for the first round), and anyone following you will need to follow where you go and do what you do. As your child follows behind you, and maybe someone behind them and so on, stop in a place where they can see how many are now in line. When they followed, the line grew in size. This is similar to how Jesus called his disciples. Read the scripture together.

Scripture to Share:

And he said to them, "Follow me, and I will make you fishers of men."
Matthew 4:19 (ESV)

Questions to Discuss:

1. How did you feel when you started following the leader?
2. Did you think that others would follow too? Why or why not?
3. What do you think it means to be a fisher of men?
4. How can we help others follow Jesus?
5. would happen if we shared Jesus with someone new every day?

The Big Picture:

We can't do anything without Jesus, and he has called us to share His good news with everyone around us!

Prayer Time:

Encourage one member of your family to pray about the following:

-Thank God that we can follow Him!

-Ask God to give us opportunities to invite others to follow Jesus, too.

-Pray that your family would be "fishers of men" and would lead others to Christ.

The Narrow Road

In this lesson, your child will learn God will be our guide.

What You'll Need:

Duct or Masking Tape

(whatever will stick to your floor without damaging it)

Instructions:

In an open space in your home, stick tape to the ground forming a straight line, long enough to be a "tightrope" your kids can walk along. Bring your kids over to the tape on the ground and read the Scripture aloud. Then, begin to explain that life with Christ is a narrow road; there will always be other options that, in most cases, are easier paths. Following Jesus will look different and can be tough at times like walking on the tape. Have them physically walk along the tape (think "the floor is lava" with this one), and celebrate when they make it to the other side.

Scripture to Share:

Enter through the narrow gate. For wide is the gate and broad is the road that leads to destruction, and many enter through it. But small is the gate and narrow the road that leads to life, and only a few find it.

Matthew 7:13-14 (NIV)

Questions to Discuss:

1. How did you feel walking across the tape?
2. Were there other ways to get to the other side? Were they bigger? Easier?
3. How does it feel knowing that walking with Jesus is a narrow road? Are you ready to walk with Him?

Parents: For helpful resources on leading your child to Christ, look into:
"I Believe in Jesus" by John MacArthur & "God's Great News for Children" by Focus on the Family/Heritage Builders

The Big Picture:

God has ordered our steps. He will guide us and save us. Jesus is the narrow gate and the narrow way, and whoever travels this path, will be saved.

Prayer Time:

Encourage one member of your family to pray about the following:

-Thank God that He has created a path for us to follow.

-Ask God to remind us He is with us when we walk the narrow road.

-Thank God for walking with us.

Be Careful Little Eyes What You See

In this lesson, your child will learn to guard their hearts and minds and focus on the things of God.

What You'll Need:

Mail from your mailbox

Instructions:

Have your child retrieve the mail with you and bring everything inside. On a flat surface, begin to look through each item and explain, "We are going to sort through the mail. Some things we will get rid of, and some things we will keep." So, the two categories are:

1) Keep 2) Toss

Sort your mail into these two piles. Begin explaining this is similar to our own lives and what we allow into our minds. Not everything we see or read is good for us to keep in our minds or hearts, and some things need to be thrown out! It's important that we guard our minds and what our eyes see every single day. It's important we focus on good things, things of God, and His Word. Read the scripture together.

Scripture to Share:

Set your minds on things that are above, not on things that are on earth.

Colossians 3:2 (ESV)

Questions to Discuss:

1. Has there been a time when you saw or read something that wasn't good for you?
2. How do we guard our minds and our eyes?
3. Why does God tell us not to focus on "things that are on earth"?
4. What are some good things that we can set our minds on?

The Big Picture:

God has called us to focus on things of Him, even when the world around us is scary or uncertain.

Prayer Time:

Encourage one member of your family to pray about the following:

-Thank God that He protects us every day!

-Ask God to show you things that aren't good for your mind.

-Pray for God's help to "toss" things that aren't good for your mind or your heart.

Vine and Branches

In this lesson, your child will learn that if we stay close to God, we will bear fruit.

What You'll Need:

1 dead or dying branch (or stem) from a tree or bush

Instructions:

Find a dead or dying branch that has fallen from a tree or bush, allowing your children to analyze it. Ultimately, note that after a short time, it dies without the "vine," its source of life. Read the scripture together.

Scripture to Share:

I am the vine; you are the branches. If a man remains in me and I in him, he will bear much fruit; apart from me you can do nothing. If anyone does not remain in me, he is like a branch that is thrown away and withers; such branches are picked up, thrown into the fire and burned.

John 15:5-6 (NIV)

Questions to Discuss:

1. How do you feel seeing that the branch died?
2. How are we like the branch when we don't live each day with God?
3. How can we "bear fruit" in our own lives?
4. What does it look like to "bear fruit" as a family?

The Big Picture:

When we stay close to God, He is close to us and helps us bear fruit in our lives.

Prayer Time:

Encourage one member of your family to pray about the following:

-Thank God for giving us life.

-Pray through the fruit of the Spirit.

-Show us how to live as a fruitful family.

Morning Mercies

In this lesson, your child will learn to be thankful to God for the things we have.

What You'll Need:

1 (or more) window(s) in your home

Instructions:

Open up all the windows around the house to let light in. Even if it's only one window, let the kids open them...make it an event! Read the scripture together.

Scripture to Share:

The steadfast love of the LORD never ceases; his mercies never come to an end; they are new every morning; great is your faithfulness.

Lamentations 3:22-23 (ESV)

Questions to Discuss:

1. How does it feel seeing the bright sun shining through the window?
2. Who tells the sun to rise every morning?
3. How can we thank God for giving us another day to wake up and see the sunrise?

The Big Picture:

God's love and faithfulness will never end.

Prayer Time:

Encourage one member of your family to pray about the following:

-Thank God for giving us today, another day!

-Thank Him for being faithful, consistent, and trustworthy every day—even with the rising sun!

-Show us how to take advantage of today, sharing your Word with others.

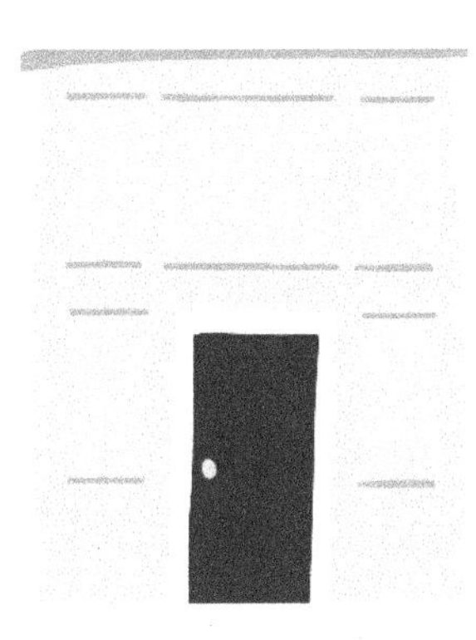

What is the Gospel?

In this lesson, your child will learn to declare the good news of Jesus.

What You'll Need:

Something to magnify your voice (a cup, your hands, a microphone, a megaphone—whatever you have in the house!)

Instructions:

Okay, parents! Prepare to join in on this one.
Use your "megaphone" and shout joyfully, loudly, and boldly throughout the house: "Jesus loves you! He died for you! God sent Him to save your soul! Follow Him and be baptized! He is the only way to eternal life!" This can seem silly, but it's the perfect example for your kids—they too may feel silly at times sharing this news in our world. They will never forget the visual of you shouting the good news through your home! Read the scriptures together.

Scripture to Share:

For God so loved the world He gave His one and only Son, that whoever believes in Him shall not perish but have eternal life.

John 3:16 (NIV)

Questions to Discuss:

1. Did you know that God sent His son, Jesus, to die for you and your sin?
2. How does it make you feel that Jesus died on a cross to save you?
3. What did Jesus save you from?
4. How can we follow Jesus?
5. How can we tell other people about Jesus?

The Big Picture:

Whoever believes that Jesus Christ is Lord and Savior of their life, and is baptized, will be saved and have eternal life.

Prayer Time:

Encourage one member of your family to pray about the following:

-Thank God for sending His Son to save us.

-Repent and apologize for your sins.

-Give us opportunities to share the Gospel with our friends and family.

-Show us how to follow Jesus as a family.

Stepping Through Seasons

In this lesson, your child will learn God will be with you through every season of life.

What You'll Need:

A path, road, or yard with both a shady spot and a sunlit spot.

Instructions:

As you walk down a path with both shade and sun, begin to explain that these factors resemble the seasons of life. Some seasons are "hotter" than others, and some are more like a nice seat in the shade to catch your breath. You may have a year that is hard. You may have a year that is easier. God brings different seasons into our lives to do different things in us and those around us. We may like certain times more than others, but through each of them, He is with us and He is in control! Read the scripture together.

Scripture to Share:

For everything there is a season, and a time for every purpose under heaven: a time to be born, and a time to die; a time to plant, and a time to pluck up that which is planted; a time to kill, and a time to heal; a time to break down, and a time to build up; a time to weep, and a time to laugh; a time to mourn, and a time to dance; a time to cast away stones, and a time to gather stones together; a time to embrace, and a time to refrain from embracing; a time to seek, and a time to lose; a time to keep, and a time to cast away; a time to rend, and a time to sew; a time to keep silence, and a time to speak; a time to love, and a time to hate; a time for war, and a time for peace... Ecclesiastes 3:1-8 (ESV)

Questions to Discuss:

1. How did you feel in the sunny spot? In the shade?
2. God knows every single year of your life already, and He knows all the things you'll do in your life. How does this make you feel?
3. When was there a time to laugh recently? And cry?

The Big Picture:

Jesus is with us in every season, good or bad.
Even when we face trouble, He has already overcome the world.

Prayer Time:

Encourage one member of your family to pray about the following:

-Thank Him for creating different seasons.

-Thank Him for being with you every year and every season of our lives.

-Ask him to help us see what He wants to teach us each year.

Knock, Knock, Who's There?

In this lesson, your child will learn God will be there for anyone that opens their heart to Him.

What You'll Need:

A door (preferably a front door with a doorbell) but any door will do!

Instructions:

First, read the Scripture together. Then, stand behind the door and have your little ones sit on the other side. Knock, and ask them if they can hear your voice from behind the door. Do they know whose voice it is without seeing you? Allow them to open the door and let you in.

Once you have walked through the open door, explain to them how this is true of God as well. He speaks to us in many different ways, knocking on the doors of our hearts. When we hear His voice, we can open our hearts to Him and let Him in. We always want to hear His voice and listen to it.

Scripture to Share:

Behold, I stand at the door and knock. If anyone hears my voice and opens the door, I will come in to him and eat with him, and he with me.

Revelation 3:20 (ESV)

Questions to Discuss:

1. Did you know who was knocking at the door before you opened it? How?
2. How did you feel once you opened the door and let them in?
3. How can we allow God to come into our hearts when He knocks?
4. How does He speak to us?

The Big Picture:

God will answer anyone who opens their heart to Him.

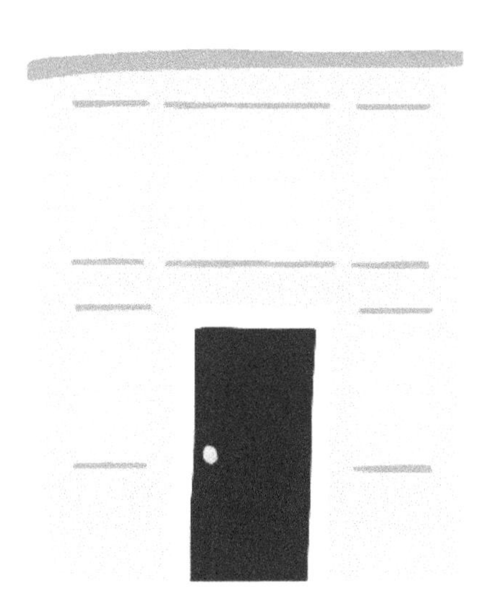

Prayer Time:

Encourage one member of your family to pray about the following:

-Thank God for a relationship with Him!

-Ask that he helps us to hear Him when He speaks to us.

-Ask him to teach us how to obey him.

A Friendly Reminder

In this lesson, your child will learn that they can listen for the Holy Spirit to guide the things they do.

What You'll Need:

An alarm clock (this can be a stand-alone clock, the one on your phone, an oven timer, etc.)

Instructions:

Prepare the kids to play a game. Have them spread out around the room and prepare to walk around the entire space quickly throughout this game. (Think of this as "freeze dance" but without the dancing. Feel free to dance if it makes it more fun for your family!) Set the alarm clock to go off every 10, 20, or 30 seconds. When it sounds, have the kids freeze wherever they are in the house. During this time, explain how the Holy Spirit, or our conscience, "reminds us" when we are doing something that is not honoring God. Just like an alarm clock reminds us (and very loudly) to do things so we don't forget, the Holy Spirit also reminds us of things. Sometimes, when we move through life so quickly, being "busy" and in a hurry, the Holy Spirit reminds us to slow down and spend time with God too. Continue this game as long as you want to. Have fun, make it your own, and allow the kids to enjoy the concept of "stopping immediately and listening" when they hear that alarm. Read the scripture together.

Scripture to Share:

In view of this, I also do my best to maintain always a blameless conscience both before God and before men.

Acts 24:16 (ESV)

Questions to Discuss:

1. Have you ever heard an alarm go off before?
2. Have you ever heard the Holy Spirit or your conscience before, reminding you that what you were doing wasn't honoring God or others? What was it?
3. What should we do when we hear the Holy Spirit next time?

The Big Picture:

God will draw near to us when we draw close to Him.

Prayer Time:

Encourage one member of your family to pray about the following:

-Thank God for giving us His Holy Spirit.

-Ask God to help us to hear and listen when He reminds us.

-Allow us to learn from what He is teaching us.

A Teeny Tiny Faith

In this lesson, your child will learn to have faith.

What You'll Need:

A tiny seed, nut or grain (chia seeds, orzo pasta, a grain of rice, a bean, a small nut—whatever you have in your home!)

Instructions:

Explain to the children what the item is you are showing them (they may not recognize it starting off). Place the item in their hands and ask: "Have you ever held anything this small in your hands?" Listen to their responses, then begin to explain that their faith may start out as tiny as what is in their hands, but God will see it. It will continue to grow and grow, but faith in Jesus is so important that even a tiny seed-sized faith is recognized by God. Begin reading the scripture together.

Scripture to Share:

And He said to them, "Because of the littleness of your faith; for truly I say to you, if you have faith the size of a mustard seed, you will say to this mountain, 'Move from here to there,' and it will move; and nothing will be impossible to you."

Matthew 17:20 (NASB)

Questions to Discuss:

1. Do you have faith the size of a mustard seed (or whatever you are using to demonstrate)? Why do you say that?
2. How does our faith grow? What do we have to do?
3. Did you know God will help grow your faith to be bigger and bigger? To trust Him more and more?

The Big Picture:

God can do a lot, even with a little faith.

Prayer Time:

Encourage one member of your family to pray about the following:

-Thank God that we can talk to Him.

-Ask Him to show us how to grow our faith every day.

-Ask Him to show us how to trust Him even with small faith.

Hosanna!

In this lesson, your child will be reminded that Jesus is the King.

Instructions:

Prepare your child to play a game. Tell them we are going to pretend the King is coming to our house in 30 minutes! With that being said, ask them what around the house needs to be done to invite the King into our home? Cleaning? Picking flowers from outside? Preparing food? Allow your child to get creative and take the reins with prepping your home for the King's arrival. Have fun with it...and set the timer! Read the scriptures together.

Scripture to Share:

When Jesus entered Jerusalem, the whole city was stirred and asked, "Who is this?" The crowds answered, "This is Jesus, the prophet from Nazareth in Galilee."

Matthew 21:10-11 (NIV)

So they took branches of palm trees and went out to meet him, crying out, "Hosanna! Blessed is he who comes in the name of the Lord, even the King of Israel!"

John 12:13 (ESV)

Questions to Discuss:

1. How did you feel knowing you were preparing your home for the King?
2. How do you think the people who saw Jesus arrive in Jerusalem felt when He arrived?
3. How did the people in Jerusalem know that Jesus was the King?
4. How can we prepare to meet with Jesus again one day?

The Big Picture:

Jesus is the Messiah, the King of Israel.
He is our Savior and our King.

Prayer Time:

Encourage one member of your family to pray about the following:

-Thank God that He is King of the world!

-Ask God to help you spend time with Him and in His Word every day.

-Thank God that He is coming again, soon!

Tell the World

In this lesson, your child will be reminded to share God's love with others.

What You'll Need:

Paper or note cards, Envelopes, Pens, crayons, or markers
(optional: stamps, stickers, candy)

Instructions:

Spend time making short notes for your neighbors about
Jesus and His love for us. Examples:
"Jesus loves you!"
"Jesus sees you and cares for you!"
"Jesus knows you by name!"
"Jesus is the way to eternal life!"
"Grace and peace to you from God our Father!"
Feel free to add pictures, stickers, or candy to take it up a notch.
Deliver a note to each mailbox in your neighborhood, or friends' houses,
or mail them out to extended family members. Read the scripture together.

Scripture to Share:

Paul, a servant of Christ Jesus, called to be an apostle and set apart for the gospel of God...To all in Rome who are loved by God and called to be his holy people: Grace and peace to you from God our Father and from the Lord Jesus Christ.

Romans 1:1, 7 (NIV)

Questions to Discuss:

1. How did you feel sending letters about Jesus to other people?
2. Did you know that Paul wrote letters telling others about Jesus too?
3. What do you hope happens when they read the letters you sent?

The Big Picture:

When your heart is changed by Jesus, you can't help but tell others about Him too!

Prayer Time:

Encourage one member of your family to pray about the following:

-Thank God for His love for us.

-Ask God to show us how to continue sharing Jesus with others.

-Thank God for the gift of salvation and that we can live our lives for Him.

Father, Son & Holy Spirit

In this lesson, your child will learn that the Father, Son, and Holy Spirit are one God and He is always with us.

What You'll Need:

1 Piece of paper (per child)

Crayons, Colored Pencils, or Markers, Scissors

Instructions:

Cut a triangle out of paper for each child. Help your children label each corner of the triangle, beginning with the top. "Father", "Son", "Holy Spirit". Allow them to draw pictures and decorate the triangle to represent each of the three persons. Read the scripture together.

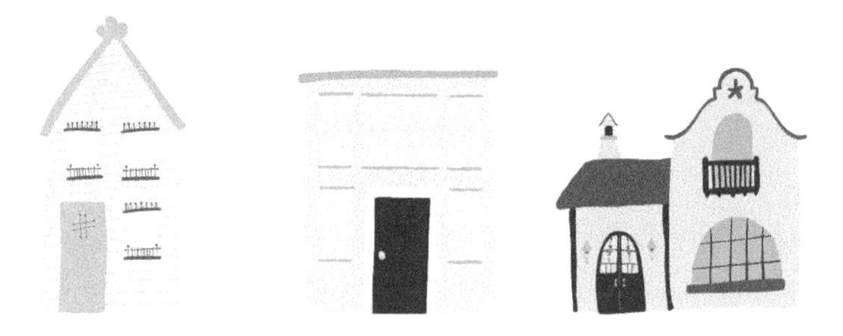

Scripture to Share:

"There are three that testify in heaven, the Father, the Word, and the Holy Spirit, and these three are one."

1 John 5:7 (MEV)

Questions to Discuss:

1. Did you know the Father, the Son, and the Holy Spirit are all one person?
2. Who is the Father? Who is His Son? Where is His Spirit?
3. How do you feel knowing that God's Spirit lives in you?

The Big Picture:

One God: Three Persons.

God has placed His Spirit within us.

He is always with us.

Prayer Time:

Encourage one member of your family to pray about the following:

-Thank God for sending His Son, Jesus.

-Thank God for sending His Holy Spirit to live in us!

-Ask God to teach us more about himself.

Feeding Our Spirit

Feeding Our Spirit In this lesson, your child will learn God guides their heart and mind when filling them with the things of God.

What You'll Need:

6-8 "healthy" Items, 6-8 "unhealthy" Items

Instructions:

Okay, parents, this one requires a little more effort on your part! Gather a box full of "healthy items" and a box full of "unhealthy items." This doesn't just apply to food!

Healthy items can be:
Sneakers (hinting at exercise and being outside)
A book (a Bible would be ideal!), Apple or Fruit, Bottle of Water, etc.

Unhealthy Items can be:
Video Games (too much time in front of a TV)
TV Remote Control, Bag of Cheetos, Stinky Socks, etc.

Stuff your mailbox with the "unhealthy items" to where it won't close all the way. Bring the kids out to the mailbox and explain that when your mind, body, and spirit are being fed (or stuffed) with things that aren't healthy for it. It will spew out, no matter what. It can spew out of your mouth (language), it can spew from your body (unhealthy/sickness), it can spew from your mind (focusing on negative or impure things), etc. Anyone can see that the mailbox is full, and it's starting to leak out bad things. This is what others can see about you, too!

Allow the kids to pull every "unhealthy" item out of the mailbox, analyze it, and ask questions. Send them back inside and now stuff the mailbox with all the "healthy items" to where it won't close.

Bring the kids back out to the mailbox, and begin to explain that when your mind, body, and spirit are being fed good things, it will overflow and everyone will be able to see it! Read the scripture together.

Scripture to Share:

Good people do good things because of the good in their hearts. Bad people do bad things because of the evil in their hearts. Your words show what is in your heart.
Luke 6:45 (CEV)

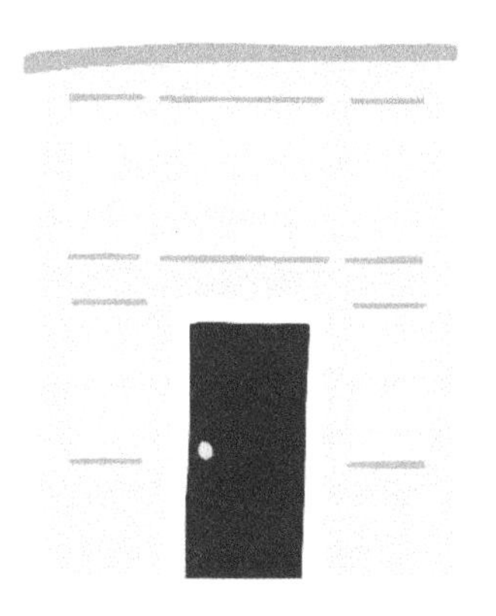

Questions to Discuss:

1. What are some healthy things you can feed your body, mind, and spirit?
2. What are unhealthy things for your body, mind, and spirit?
3. God sees what you feed your body, mind, and spirit. How does this make you feel?

The Big Picture:

God will guard our hearts and minds when we focus on things above and on Him.

Prayer Time:

Encourage one member of your family to pray about the following:

-Thank God for the fruits of the Spirit.

-Ask God to guard our hearts and minds.

-Ask God to help you fill your body, mind, and spirit with healthy things, starting today!

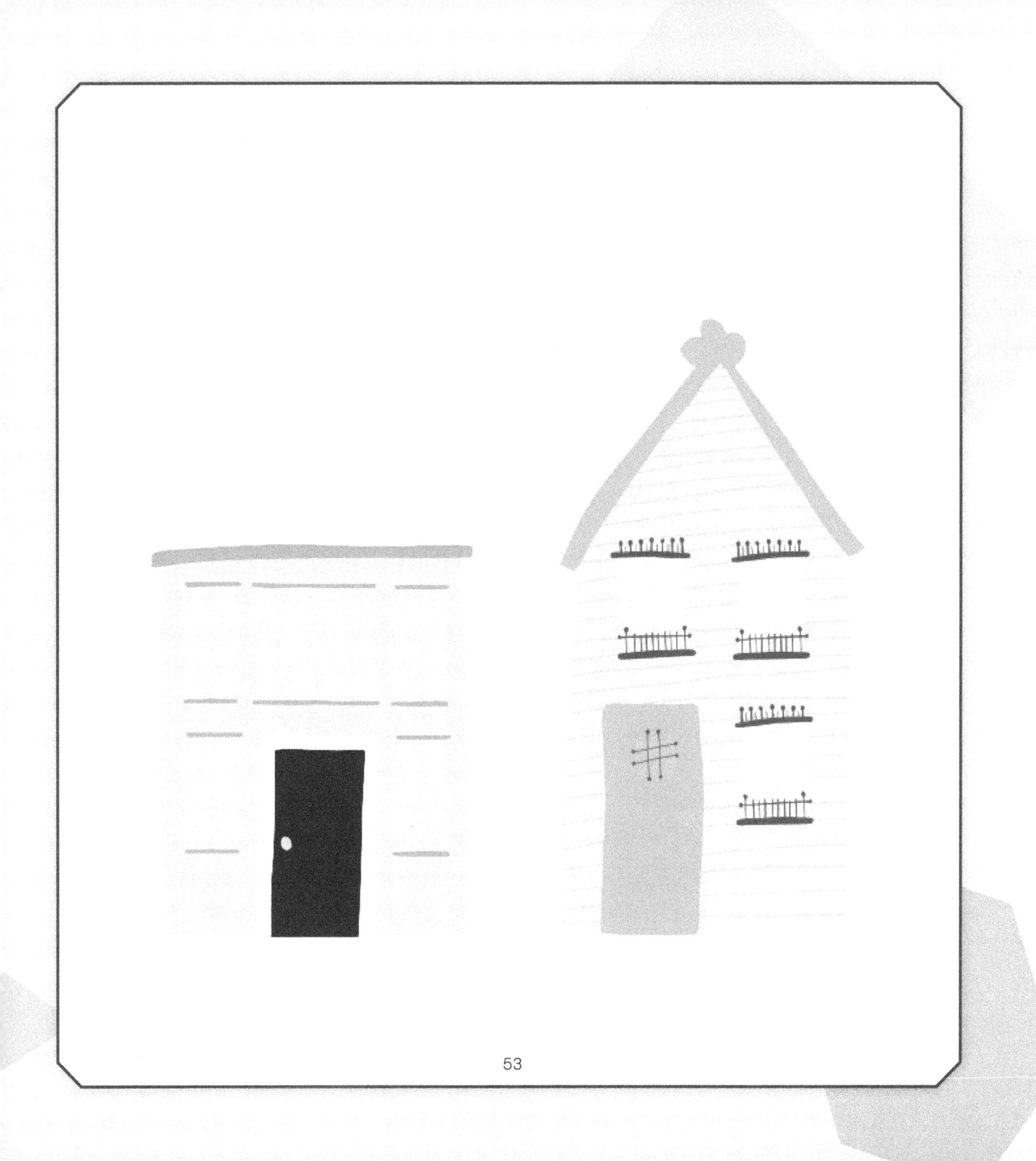

Standing Up for our Faith

In this lesson, your child will learn God will save those that stand in Him.

What You'll Need:

All you need is yourselves for this one!

Instructions:

Have your child stand in front of you. The goal of this game is for your child to remain standing until the end. Begin to lightly tug and try to move their arms or legs, pretending you are trying to knock them over. Have them shout, "I will not be shaken!" as they resist your attempts to knock them over. Once they "win" by standing until the end, explain that those who stand firm in their faith until the end will be saved. They just experienced a physical example but help them connect the dots to how it applies to their spiritual walk.

Read the scripture together.

Scripture to Share:

Be on your guard. Stand firm in the faith. Be courageous. Be strong.

1 Corinthians 16:13 (NLT)

Questions to Discuss:

1. How did you feel knowing someone was trying to knock you down?
2. How did you feel when you stood through the tugging and shaking the entire time?
3. How do we stand firm in our faith until the end?
4. What happens to those who stand firm? What happens to those who don't?

The Big Picture:

God will save those who have faith in Him.
He will save those who stand firm to the end.

Prayer Time:

Encourage one member of your family to pray about the following:

-Thank God for saving us!

-Ask God to teach us how to stand firm, even when it feels hard to do so.

-Ask God to strengthen us so we can help others stand firm, too.

A Free Gift

In this lesson, your child will learn to share the gift of Jesus with others.

What You'll Need:

1 Item per child that they would be excited to receive as a gift
(Preferably something new, but it can be small or from a dollar store!)

Instructions:

This one requires a little planning ahead, parents! Even if it's from a dollar store, pick out something your child would get really excited about receiving as a gift. Plan an uninterrupted time to present your child with this gift and explain that there was nothing they did to "earn" the gift. Read the Scripture aloud, and explain that this is true of each of us with Jesus. He gave us the gift of a relationship with Him through salvation and eternal life with Him, and we did nothing to earn it! Jesus tells us to share this same gift with others since we received it freely. Remind your child that they did nothing to deserve the gift, and they don't "need" it, but someone else may! Ask your child who they would like to give it away to for free. Listen to their responses. Read the scripture together.

Scripture to Share:

These twelve Jesus sent out with the following instructions: "Do not go among the Gentiles or enter any town of the Samaritans. Go rather to the lost sheep of Israel. As you go, proclaim this message: 'The kingdom of heaven has come near.' Heal the sick, raise the dead, cleanse those who have leprosy, drive out demons. Freely you have received; freely give. Matthew 10:5-8 (NIV)

Questions to Discuss:

1. How did it feel receiving the gift from your parent(s)?
2. How did it feel to give it away to someone else?
3. Did you know God gave you a gift? For free?
4. How can you also share this gift God gave you with others?

The Big Picture:

When we receive God's gift to us and accept Him as our Lord and Savior, we will be saved and have eternal life with Him.

Prayer Time:

Encourage one member of your family to pray about the following:

-Thank God for the amazing gift He gave us: salvation!

-Thank God that He freely gave it to us and that we didn't have to pay for our sins.

-Ask God to show us people with whom to share His gift and His Word!

In His Image

In this lesson, your child will be reminded that God created everything including them. They are wonderfully made.

What You'll Need:

1 magnifying glass

Instructions:

Use the magnifying glass to explore things both big and small. Start outside with bugs, leaves, and anything your child finds interesting. Study the intricacies of each item. Then, begin to study yourselves: the hairs on your arms, the detail of your eyes, your fingerprints. Explain that God created each item you are looking at as unique and special. He created us from inside the womb with all of these special details—no one has them but you! He cares for us so much that He spent time making each of us differently, and he cares for each of us. Read the scripture together.

Scripture to Share:

So God created man in his own image, in the image of God created them; male and female he created them.

Genesis 1:27 (NIV)

Questions to Discuss:

1. What was your favorite thing you looked at under the magnifying glass? Why?
2. How does it make you feel knowing that God made you and knows every detail about you?
3. How can we thank God for creating us each to be special in our own ways?

The Big Picture:

God knows us inside and out. He knows every hair on our heads and already knows what we will do every day we live.

Prayer Time:

Encourage one member of your family to pray about the following:

-Thank God for His Creation.

-Thank God for creating us uniquely.

-Pray we never lose the awe and wonder of His creation.

Our Faithful Friend

In this lesson, your child will be reminded God is always with them.

What You'll Need:

1 piece of paper per child, Crayons, colored pencils, or markers

Instructions:

Have your child draw a picture of their best friend. Hang on to these drawings until the questions segment of this lesson. Read and discuss the scripture.

Scripture to Share:

Be strong and courageous. Do not be afraid or terrified because of them, for the LORD your God goes with you; he will never leave you nor forsake you.

Deuteronomy 31:6 (NIV)

Questions to Discuss:

1.Who is your best friend?

2. Why did you draw this person?

3. Did you know that God is the best friend anyone could have?

4. How do we know that God is faithful?

The Big Picture:

God knows us inside and out. He knows every hair on our heads and already knows what we will do every day we live.

*Have your children turn over their sheet of paper and now draw Jesus as their best friend!

Prayer Time:

Encourage one member of your family to pray about the following:

-Thank God for His faithfulness!

-Thank God that we can call Him our friend.

-Ask God to teach us how to be faithful to Him more and more every day.

I Am His

In this lesson, your child will learn they are created in the image of God.

What You'll Need:

1 piece of paper per child, Crayons, colored pencils, or markers

Instructions:

Have your child sit and prepare to draw a picture. Read the Scripture aloud.Emphasize that your children are "chosen, royalty, created by God, you're created in His image, etc." Have them draw what comes to mind when they hear these things. Allow them to fill the page with reminders and visuals of this Scripture. Hang their drawing on their door, mirror, or somewhere they can see it for the rest of the week! Read the scripture together.

Scripture to Share:

But you are a chosen race, a royal priesthood, a holy nation, a people for his own possession, that you may proclaim the excellencies of him who called you out of darkness into his marvelous light.

1 Peter 2:9 (ESV)

Questions to Discuss:

1.Who does God say you are?

2. What did you like about drawing your picture?

3. Do you have any questions?

The Big Picture:

God created us in His image, and He saved us from darkness.

Prayer Time:

Encourage one member of your family to pray about the following:

-Thank God for creating us in His image.

-Thank God for choosing us and saving us.

-Ask God to show us ways to share this news with others.

The BIBLE

In this lesson, your child will learn the importance of reading the Bible and praying.

What You'll Need:

1 Bible

Instructions:

Have everyone sit close together. Turn to the table of contents. If your children can read, allow them to read aloud the names of each book in the Bible. Remind them they are holding the most important book ever written and that we are lucky we have one (or more) in our home. Some families in other countries would do anything to have their own Bible. Remind them that this book is God-breathed, meaning every word is from Him. Reading the Bible every day is important. We want to remember it better than we know our phone number or our favorite restaurant order. Read the scripture together.

Scripture to Share:

All Scripture is God-breathed and is useful for teaching, rebuking, correcting and training in righteousness, so that the servant of God may be thoroughly equipped for every good work.

2 Timothy 3:16-17 (NIV)

Questions to Discuss:

1.How did you feel holding the Bible?

2. Why is it important to read the Bible?

3. What can we learn from the Bible?

4. Do you have a favorite verse, story, or book from the Bible?

5. Why do we pray?

6. Is there anyone you would like to pray for now?

The Big Picture:

God hears those who call on Him and listens to those who make requests.

Prayer Time:

Encourage one member of your family to pray about the following:

-Thank God for His Word.

-Thank God that we can talk to Him through prayer.

-Ask Him to help us pray with more faith every day.

Who Do I Reflect?

In this lesson, your child will learn when we live for God, He will guide us.

What You'll Need:

1 hand mirror or a front-facing camera on a cell phone and 1 Bible

Instructions:

Have your children take turns holding the mirror. Have them look at themselves in it and notice what they focus on. Have each child hold the mirror in front of their face (reflecting themselves) and have them begin to walk forward. Keeping the mirror directly in front of their face, they should experience trouble seeing what is ahead of them as they walk.

Now, have them hold the mirror out in front of them, but point the reflection to the ceiling. Have them walk forward, as they can see directly what is in front of them. This should be much easier than the first time they tried to walk.

Remind them that in life, when we only live for ourselves and only reflect on ourselves, we will always stumble. When we live for God, our hands are open and extended to those around us and to God as He leads us. Read the scripture together.

Scripture to Share:

As all of us reflect the glory of the Lord with unveiled faces, we are becoming more like him with ever-increasing glory by the Lord's Spirit.

2 Corinthians 3:18 (ISV)

Questions to Discuss:

1.Was it difficult walking with the mirror in front of your face?

2. How was it walking with the mirror pointed upwards?

3. Who did the mirror reflect when it was pointed in front of you?

4. Who did the mirror reflect when you pointed it outward and upward?

The Big Picture:

When we live for God, He will guide our steps. When we live for ourselves, we begin walking without God and may stumble.

Prayer Time:

Encourage one member of your family to pray about the following:

-Thank God for His guidance in our lives.

-Ask God to show us new ways to reflect who He is to the world.

-Ask God to show you who you are currently reflecting.

Planting A Seed

In this lesson, your child will learn when we root our faith in good soil and take care of it, it will grow.

What You'll Need:

1 pot per child, Potting soil (or dirt from outside), 1 seed per child, Water (in a watering can or cup)

Instructions:

Have your child place soil in their pot. Then, have them plant the seed firmly into the soil and water it. Have them place their pot in the sunlight and observe any growth over the next few weeks! Explain that when they choose good soil and they water and care for the seed, it will begin to grow! The same is true of our faith. Read the scriptures together.

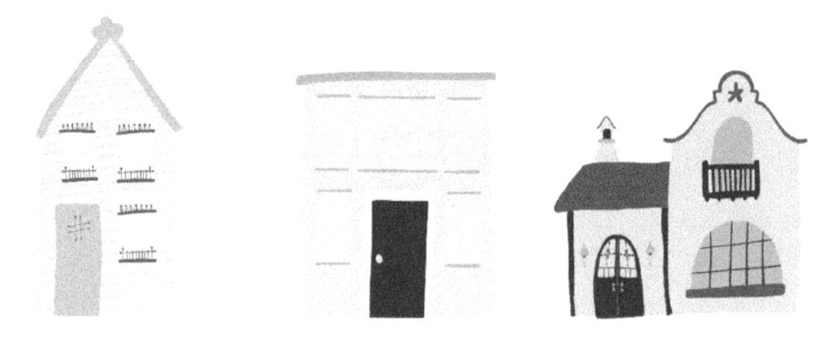

Scripture to Share:

As he was scattering the seed, some fell along the path, and the birds came and ate it up. Some fell on rocky places, where it did not have much soil. It sprang up quickly, because the soil was shallow. But when the sun came up, the plants were scorched, and they withered because they had no root. Other seed fell among thorns, which grew up and choked the plants. Still other seed fell on good soil, where it produced a crop—a hundred, sixty or thirty times what was sown.

"Listen then to what the parable of the sower means: When anyone hears the message about the kingdom and does not understand it, the evil one comes and snatches away what was sown in their heart. This is the seed sown along the path. The seed falling on rocky ground refers to someone who hears the word and at once receives it with joy. But since they have no root, they last only a short time. When trouble or persecution comes because of the word, they quickly fall away. The seed falling among the thorns refers to someone who hears the word, but the worries of this life and the deceit-

fulness of wealth choke the word, making it unfruitful. But the seed falling on good soil refers to someone who hears the word and understands it. This is the one who produces a crop, yielding a hundred, sixty or thirty times what was sown."

Matthew 13:4-7; 18-23 (NIV)

Questions to Discuss:

1.How did you feel when you finished planting your seed?

2. Are you excited to watch it grow? Will you keep taking care of it? Watering it?

3. How does our faith grow like that little seed?

4. How can we "water" or grow our faith?

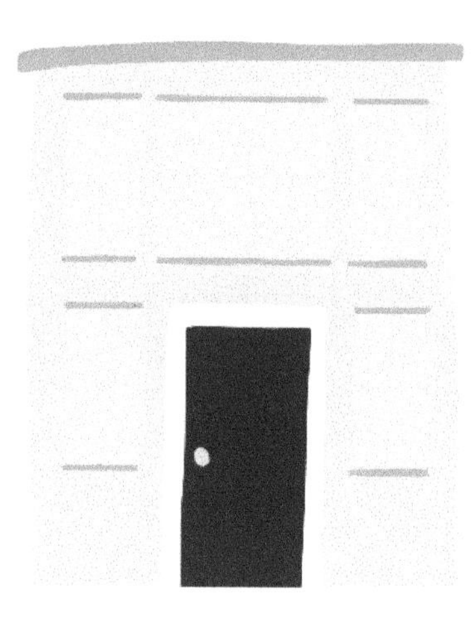

The Big Picture:

When we root our faith in good soil, it will grow.

Prayer Time:

Encourage one member of your family to pray about the following:

-Thank God for His Word.

-Ask God to help water and grow your faith.

-Ask God to show you if there is anything in the way of your faith getting stronger.

God With Us

In this lesson, your child will be reminded that God is always with them.

What You'll Need:

1 candle , A lighter or matches

Instructions:

Set a candle in the middle of a table and dim the lights. Have everyone gather around the unlit candle. Remind your children that "God is the light of the world. Even when things in life seem dark or troublesome, He is always with us. We light this candle as a reminder that He is here, right now, with us." Sit around the lit candle and continue the lesson. Read the scripture together.

Scripture to Share:

Fear not, for I am with you; be not dismayed, for I am your God; I will strengthen you, I will help you, I will uphold you with my righteous right hand.
Isaiah 41:10 (ESV)

Questions to Discuss:

1. How do you feel knowing God is with you right now?
2. Is there anywhere you will go that God won't be with you?
3. Did you know that we can be a light in this world?
4. How can we share His light with others?

The Big Picture:

God is always with us. He is never far.
He will never leave us.

Prayer Time:

Encourage one member of your family to pray about the following:

-Thank God that He is always with us.
-Ask God to help you shine His light to the world.
-Thank God that He is the Light of the World.

It's A Prayer Party

In this lesson, your child will learn how to pray.

What You'll Need:

All you need is yourselves for this one!

Instructions:

This exercise is all about practicing prayer. It can be short and simple but allow your kids to see and hear you praying a prayer. Encourage them that they can do it too! Have everyone sit close together and hold hands. Begin praying out loud. Thank God for the gift of His word. Thank Him for each person in the room with you. Pray for other people, their needs, their health, and their faith. Allow others to join in the rest of this prayer time, "popcorn style." Read the scripture together.

Scripture to Share:

Therefore confess your sins to each other and pray for each other so that you may be healed. The prayer of a righteous person is powerful and effective.

James 5:16 (NIV)

Questions to Discuss:

1. How did you feel praying out loud?
2. Did you know that God hears you every time you pray? Even silently?
3. Who can you pray for today?

The Big Picture:

Prayer is powerful.

God hears our prayers.

Prayer is how we talk with God.

Prayer Time:

Encourage one member of your family to pray about the following:

-Thank God that we can talk with him through prayer.

-Pray for someone who doesn't know Jesus.

-Ask God to grow your prayer life with Him!

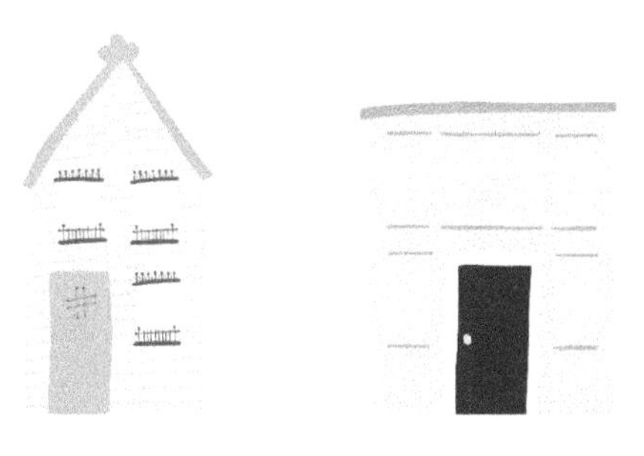

Provider & Sustainer

In this lesson, your child will learn God will provide.

What You'll Need:

Table, Silverware, Plates, Cups

Instructions:

Prepare your child to help you set the table (even if it's not for a meal). Feel free to make this as simple or extravagant as you want to! As you set the table together, begin explaining that your food and meals, your money, your home, and your family are all gifts God has given to you. Any time we eat together, we give thanks to God for all He has given us. Read the scripture together.

Scripture to Share:

Consider the ravens: they neither sow nor reap, they have neither storehouse nor barn, and yet God feeds them. Of how much more value are you than the birds!

Luke 12:24 (ESV)

Questions to Discuss:

1. How does it make you feel knowing God gave you everything you have?
2. God cares for you and will always provide for you. Why do you think He does this?
3. How can we thank God for all He has blessed us with?
4. How can we share the gifts God gave us with others?

The Big Picture:

God is our provider. He is good and gives good gifts.

Prayer Time:

Encourage one member of your family to pray about the following:

-Thank God for all He has given us.

-Ask God to remind you that He is in control.

-Thank God for always providing what we need and when we need it.

Prince of Peace

In this lesson, your child will learn that in Jesus, they can find peace and comfort.

What You'll Need:

1 large blanket, (Picnic snacks, toys, or music is optional)

Instructions:

The goal of this activity is to create a peaceful picnic. Lay your blanket out in the grass, and enjoy food or snacks, toys, or music together while outside. Lie on the blanket and gaze up at the sky, admiring the clouds, being quiet, and embracing stillness. Talk about this peaceful moment that's been created and how each person feels lying there.

Read the scripture together.

Scripture to Share:

The Lord is my shepherd, I lack nothing.

He makes me lie down in green pastures,
He leads me beside quiet waters,

He refreshes my soul. He guides me along
the right paths for His name's sake.

Even though I walk through the darkest valley,
I will fear no evil, for you are with me;
your rod and your staff, they comfort me.

You prepare a table before me in the presence of my enemies.
You anoint my head with oil; my cup overflows.

Surely your goodness and love will follow me all the days of my life,
and I will dwell in the house of the Lord forever.

Psalm 23 (NIV)

Questions to Discuss:

1. How did you feel relaxing and looking at the sky?
2. Have you ever had a time when God comforted you?
3. How can you ask God for His peace any time you are scared or anxious?

The Big Picture:

God is the Prince of Peace. In Him, we have everything we need.

Prayer Time:

Encourage one member of your family to pray about the following:

-Thank God that He is with us!

-Thank God for His peace and His comfort.

-Ask God to refresh our souls today.

I Know You

In this lesson, your child will learn that even though we can't see God, he is there for them.

What You'll Need:

1 Blindfold (Scarf, Bandana, etc)

Instructions:

Blindfold one child at a time, only covering their eyes. Instruct them to listen as you guide them through your home (or outside) and have them walk toward the sound of your voice. Remind them that even though they can't see you, they can hear you and know your voice well. Once they reach you or get close enough, take the blindfold off and begin the lesson. Read the scripture with them.

Scripture to Share:

So we fix our eyes not on what is seen, but on what is unseen, since what is seen is temporary, but what is unseen is eternal.

2 Corinthians 4:18 (NIV)

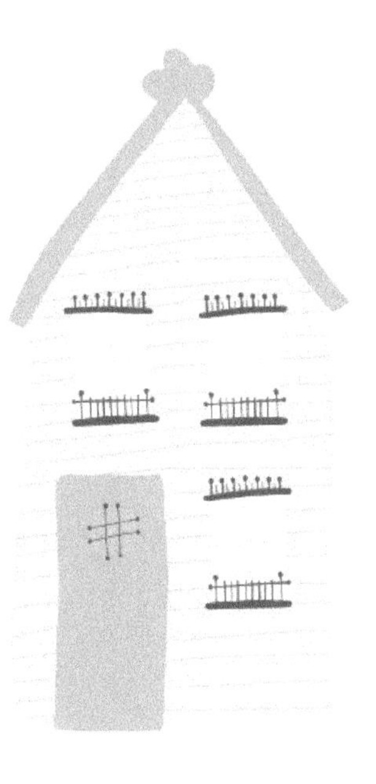

Questions to Discuss:

1. How did you feel knowing you couldn't see who was guiding you?
2. Even though you couldn't see them, did you know who was leading you? Did you trust them?
3. Did you know that God is always leading us? What does this mean?
4. Even though you can't see Him, God speaks to us—do you know His voice? How do you know it?

The Big Picture:

Even though we can't see God, He speaks to us, and we can recognize His voice.

Prayer Time:

Encourage one member of your family to pray about the following:

-Thank God that He speaks to us!

-Ask God to help you recognize His voice.

-Pray you will trust where He leads you, even when you can't see it.

Your Kingdom, Not Mine

In this lesson, your child will learn that God's kingdom will last forever.

What You'll Need:

Building Blocks, Jenga Blocks, or Legos (really, anything stackable!)

Instructions:

Have a competition to see who can build the biggest, baddest, best "kingdom" of blocks. Take time to allow your children to be creative and have fun with this activity. Once they have finished building, begin to explain that in our world, people will build kingdoms for themselves however they can with money, cars, jobs, popularity, houses, vacations—anything that gives them more of what the world has to offer. But the Bible says, "Your Kingdom come, Your will be done..."(Matthew 6:10, NIV), which means, we need to build God's kingdom and not our own. Instruct your children to completely topple their "kingdoms." Now, have them build one giant kingdom together and have them imagine it's "the Kingdom of God."

Scripture to Share:

Your kingdom come, your will be done, on earth as it is in heaven.

Matthew 6:10 (NIV)

Questions to Discuss:

1.How did it feel when you saw your "kingdom" fall to the ground?

2. How can we help build God's kingdom?

3. How does it feel knowing you can help build the Kingdom of God?

The Big Picture:

God's Kingdom will reign forever.

Prayer Time:

Encourage one member of your family to pray about the following:

-Thank God that we can be part of building His Kingdom.

-Ask God to show you if you are building your own Kingdom in your life.

-Ask God to help you "knock over" anything in your life that needs to go so you can focus on Him.

Eternal Life Through Him

In this lesson, your child will learn about heaven.

What You'll Need:

1 Blank Sheet of Paper per child, Colored pencils, markers, or crayons

Instructions:

Have your child draw what they imagine Heaven will be like. Allow them to get creative, using imagination and descriptions. Once they have completed their illustration, begin reading through the Scripture.

Scripture to Share:

Then the angel showed me the river of the water of life, bright as crystal, flowing from the throne of God and of the Lamb through the middle of the street of the city; also, on either side of the river, the tree of life with its twelve kinds of fruit, yielding its fruit each month. The leaves of the tree were for the healing of the nations. No longer will there be anything accursed, but the throne of God and of the Lamb will be in it, and his servants will worship him. They will see his face, and his name will be on their foreheads. And night will be no more. They will need no light of lamp or sun, for the Lord God will be their light, and they will reign forever and ever.

Revelation 22:1-5 (NIV)

Questions to Discuss:

1.Did you know that Jesus is King in Heaven forever?

2. What do you think it will be like to live there?

3. How do we get to Heaven?

The Big Picture:

God will reign forever in Heaven. Anyone who believes in Jesus and is saved will spend the rest of eternity in Heaven with God.

Prayer Time:

Encourage one member of your family to pray about the following:

-Thank God for the gift of eternal life

-Ask God to show you ways to share His love with others, so that they would know Him and be saved.

-Pray that anyone who doesn't know Jesus would come to know Him and spend eternity in Heaven with Him.

Notes

MacArthur, John. I Believe in Jesus. Nashville, TN: Tommy Nelson, a division of Thomas Nelson, 2016.

Osborne, Rick, and Marnie Wooding. God's Great News for Children: Leading Your Child to Christ. Wheaton, IL: Tyndale House, 2002.

Acknowledgements

To the Lord, for birthing this content through a season of transition and encouraging me to take the next step with it. I pray it honors, glorifies and transforms many hearts and many homes in Jesus' name.

To my husband, Taylor, for the endless support and listening to every idea as it was fleshed out. I am thankful to have you speaking into this project and can't wait to walk through it with our own little family.

To United House Publishing, for pushing to make this vision come to life and challenging me to go deeper throughout the publication process.

About the Author

Leah met Jesus in elementary school and since has been serving in ministry through leading worship over the last 15 years.

She grew up in South Florida and she now lives in Tallahassee, FL with her husband and their two young boys. (bless.)

Leah wrote "Make His House Your Home" after leaving full time staff at Elevation Church to stay home. She sensed God was leading her to begin writing for her own children.

Leah has a heart for new moms and the role they carry in leading their children to live Godly lives. Now she is able to share these lessons with parents across the country all with one mission in mind: making Christ known, starting at home.

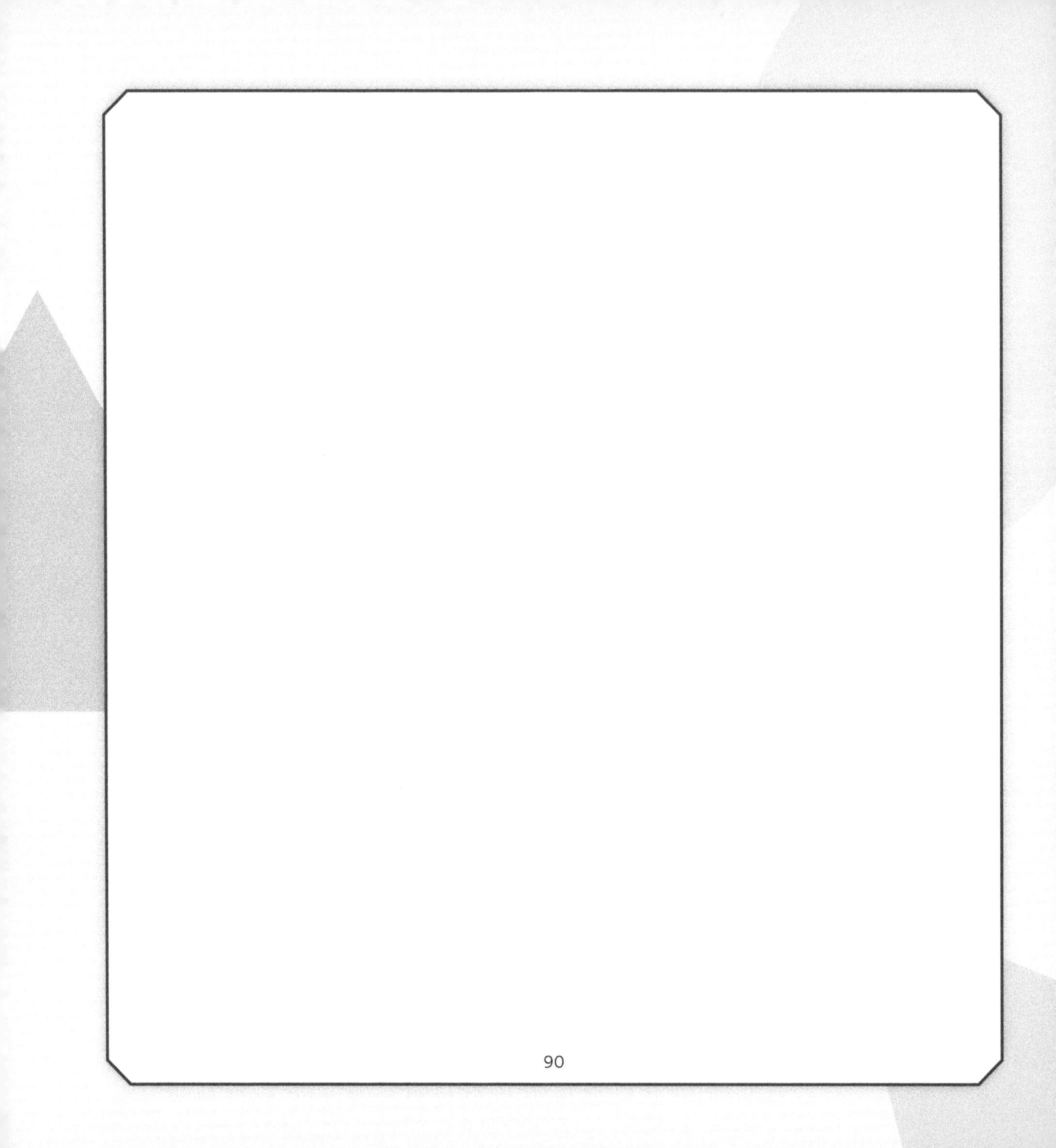

CPSIA information can be obtained
at www.ICGtesting.com
Printed in the USA
BVHW020949230622
640494BV00007B/358

9 781952 840241